The Thoughts
of
Nanushka

Volumes I—VI

To Liz

Best Wishes for 1996.

Read & Enjoy.

With Love   Carolyn & Neil XX.

The Thoughts
of
Nanushka

Volumes I—VI

Nan Witcomb

THE THOUGHTS OF NANUSHKA VOL I-VI
In one volume
Yesterday, Today and Tomorrow
Loving and Living
This Moment is Forever
Between Love and Loneliness
Pocketful of Dreams
The Wonder of Tomorrow
ISBN 0 9598294 8 2
Sketches: Bruce Swann
© Copyright Nan Witcomb September 1979
Reprinted May 1980, May 1981, May 1982, October 1983, May 1984, February 1985,
January 1987, March 1988, August 1988, May 1989, July 1990, March 1991,
October 1991, October 1992, November 1993, September 1994
Previously published in separate volumes
© Copyright Nan Witcomb
1971, 1972, 1973, 1974, 1976, 1978

THE THOUGHTS OF NANUSHKA VOL VII-XII
In one volume
Love, Tears and Dreams
Rainbows are for Everyone
After the Loving
Once upon a Memory
Gift of Love
Tears and Tenderness
ISBN 0 949332 03 8
Sketches: Fiona Heysen
© Copyright Nan Witcomb January 1987
Reprinted March 1988, August 1988, May 1989, July 1990, March 1991,
October 1991, October 1992, November 1993, September 1994
Volumes VII-XII previously published as 3 separate volumes
VOL VII-VIII © Copyright Nan Witcomb September 1980
Reprinted October 1981, October 1982, May 1984, February 1985, May 1985
VOL IX-X © Copyright Nan Witcomb October 1983
Reprinted May 1984, May 1985
VOL XI-XII © Copyright Nan Witcomb October 1985

THE THOUGHTS OF NANUSHKA VOL XIII-XIV
In one volume
The Understanding Heart
Colours of Love
ISBN 0 949332 07 0
Sketches: Boris Franco
© Copyright Nan Witcomb April 1990
Reprinted April 1992, November 1993
Volumes XIII-XIV previously printed as 2 separate volumes
VOL XIII © Copyright Nan Witcomb January 1988
VOL XIV © Copyright Nan Witcomb July 1989

THE THOUGHTS OF NANUSHKA VOL XV-XVI
In one volume
Beyond the Loving
Ride on a Rainbow
ISBN 0 949332 10 0
Sketches: Boris Franco
© Copyright Nan Witcomb September 1994
Volumes XV-XVI previously printed as 2 separate volumes
VOL XV © Copyright Nan Witcomb April 1991
Reprinted September 1993
VOL XVI © Copyright Nan Witcomb September 1992

Please direct enquiries to—
Nan Witcomb, P.O. Box 230, Brighton S.A. 5048

By the same author: Up Here and Down There—Air Hostess stories

Printed at Gillingham Printers Pty Ltd, 153 Holbrooks Road, Underdale, S.A.

For my friends –

without you
Nanushka does not exist –
her thoughts
belong to you

Nan Witcomb

Yesterday, Today and Tomorrow

IF I love
I will love beyond today –
beyond the sensuous tingling of the body –
beyond the imprisoned slavery of the mind –
I will love freely
as love was meant to be –
like the white wings of a gull
on a journey to the sun –
like the wonder of tomorrow
and the wonder of a thousand tomorrows
with the faith of a thousand yesterdays
which have freed me
to love this way –

CHRISTMAS should be
people giving –
Christmas should be
people loving –
Christmas should be
every day of the year . . . . .

I heard them talking of their tomorrow –
beautiful people –
talking of life and love,
of war and death
and changing the world –
circles of conversation
like goldfish in a bowl
going nowhere –
I thought of yesterday
and didn't have the heart to tell them
we were the beautiful people then –
trying to change the world –
and our circles of conversation
were like goldfish in a bowl
going nowhere . . . . .

I wish I could make you understand –
there is a whole big, beautiful world here –
ready for us to live in –
not wishes for tomorrow
nor memories of yesterday –
but **now** –
a billion fleeting moments
merging together
to make a life time –
Love this moment
and it is forever –
I wish I could make you understand . . . . .

Young—
but with the wisdom of forever –
peaceful as the quiet beyond the sky,
Lonely –
yet sharing in a world of other people –
seeing life
through other peoples' eyes –
Afraid –
but braver than tomorrow,
wondering if what is
will always be –
borrowing your happiness and sorrow
with the unrequited freedom of the free –
Sad –
as Autumn snowdrift in the valley,
eyes with unshed tears too proud to fall –
A heart that trusts in love
but not in loving –
yet knowing all the while
that love is all –

SOMETIMES I wish I could be
right inside the minds
of the ones I love –
What would I do?
probably nothing –
just dwell there
and watch them
going mad –

WHAT is love?
Is it a passing fever of the body,
which, like hunger, can be satisfied –
only to return again –
a million times stronger
under the guise of love?
Is it a power over the mind?
tentacles that creep upon the innocent –
an insidious phantom
stealing unseen and unsuspected
upon the willing victim,
sucking out life's blood
and sapping the will
under the guise of love?
So what is love?
To me it is a simple thing,
tender as the petals of a camellia
yet strong as the roots of a willow tree –
love is truth –
and love unadorned
is what I give to you . . . . .
for what it's worth . . . . .

PLEASE do not exhaust me
with your temperament,
nor wring my heart
with unnecessary tears –
for even the most peaceful soul
can be tormented out of it's serenity
into a raging inferno
that burns love
to a cold, grey ash . . . . .

A tree that stands
bereft of leaves,
all gnarled and knotted
as befalls a thing that breathes –
grey, alone and stark,
impervious to wind or rain or dark,
older than time itself
and past the care
of love or hate
or even self despair –
but where the roots lie anchored
deep and warm,
a seed is flung in anger
by the storm –
and there together in the sun,
the old tree and the seed
grow into one.

ONE bed –
One pillow –
Two souls
who understand
what's left of the night
is precious –
because this night
will never be again . . . . .

WAS it only yesterday we found
the little white rabbit
lying still upon the ground?
All through the happy summer
unaware,
our carefree furry visitor
had played without a care –
and loving one another,
you and I,
had laughed and played,
not thinking of 'goodbye' –
The little white rabbit,
you and I, my friend –
we did not know
the summer has to end . . . . .

I heard you laugh today –
from your heart –
like springs of water
released at last
from the deep unknown of you –
I smiled and was glad
you were happy –
then wondered why
I never made you laugh that way –
I suppose it's because
I cared too much . . . . .

WHO makes the rules?
Who says where duty ends
and life begins?
Can passion be a bore?
Perhaps we have been taught too well
that love is just another chore –

WE knew our love could never be,
for like the golden sand,
the more you try to hold it tight
the more escapes your hand –
The mighty plans of mice and men
will often go astray –
and what was so a year ago
may not be so today –
We're born into a changing world,
the young too soon grow old
and storm clouds in a summer sky
can make the day grow cold –
And though our love can never be –
for love's like golden sand –
you'll know through all eternity
that I will understand –
The time may go –
the winds may blow
and restless is the sea –
but you will know I'll understand
through all eternity –

I walked on our beach today –
alone – except for my footprints
tagging along behind
like a faithful puppy dog –
stopping when I did –
following –
but even they didn't stay long;
the cold west wind
blew a blizzard of fine white sand
around my feet
until my footprints
faded back into the beach again –
like a memory
of the summer before last . . . . .

I'LL fill my nights and days,
so not to think of you –
and look up friends I haven't seen in years –
I'll read sad books and watch sad films
to camouflage my tears –
I'll play the clown
and drink too much,
trying to forget
the way your hand caressed a glass
or held a cigarette –
but in the lonely light of dawn,
when dreams are hard to hold,
the foolish mask has slipped away,
the truth is stark and cold –
I'll touch the pillow where you slept
and in my heart I'll smile –
remembering you loved me . . . . .
for a while . . . . .

HAVE I really learned my lesson?
Shall I run when someone says,
"Please help me – I need you –
Please be kind" –
Shall I pretend I didn't hear them
and go upon my way –
will it make the slightest difference
if I stay . . . . . ?

Don't make me fall in love again,
don't let your hand touch mine,
don't make that old familiar thrill
start tingling in my spine –
Don't make the nights rush by again
and all the days seem long –
don't fill my earth and sky again –
let one of us be strong.
Don't make me talk about you,
just to say your name aloud
or let my eyes betray me
when I see you in a crowd –
Don't make me fall in love again,
please let my heart decide
that this is just another game,
a roller coaster ride –
but who knows where a love begins
or how a game might end –
and maybe somewhere in between
I'll fall in love again . . . . .

I would touch your hand in friendship
and ride upon your smile,
I would warm my travelling heart
before your fire –
but have I loved too well, too often –
is my gypsy soul afraid
of drowning
in your understanding eyes . . . . . ?

. . . . . people laughing, people crying,
babies born and old men dying,
the endless circle turns another turn –
Ever changing – colours blending,
no beginning – without ending –
we live and learn
forgetting what we learn –
Is it right or is it wrong for
us to sing and who's the song for?
the endless circle turns another turn –
Is it wrong or is it right for
us to fight and what we fight for?
we live and learn
forgetting what we learn –
Loving, hating, joy and sorrow,
yesterday, today, tomorrow –
the endless circle turns another turn –
Like a mist upon the mountain,
like a never-ending fountain –
We live and learn –
forgetting what we learn . . . . .

WALK bravely
into the mystery of tomorrow –
Somewhere in the dim, green maybe
there lives a spark of beginning
called truth –
Believe it –
and the dim, green maybe
becomes
the shining **is**.

I loved the rich green grass of life
and sometimes, mornings in the early Spring,
upon a frosty, virgin strip of green
I've walked – not knowing I was trespassing –
I trod upon the rich green grass of life,
my mind somewhere a million miles away,
not knowing that my footprints in the frost
might mar the first bright innocence of day –
And in the summer when the grass grew tall,
I'd make a soft, green pillow for your head
and loving one another, you and I
would use the cool sweet meadow for our bed –
But now in the Autumn of my life,
the past, like a misty, half forgotten tune,
I wonder if we'd trodden with more care –
would the rich, green grass of life have died so soon?
I've loved the rich green grass of life
and sometimes, mornings in the early Spring,
we watch the children running through the field,
not knowing they are trespassing –
And so in the winter of my life,
I'll know, as I know the young one day grow old –
our footprints do not matter in the end,
and the rich green grass of life will turn to gold . . . . .

Loving and Living

No matter
what I may become,
for better
or for worse –
at least
I am a human being –

Love is like an orange –
give it away
when it is green,
and it could end
in the gutter
half eaten and discarded –
keep it too long
and who wants
the dry and withered fruit?
So give it carefully, my friend,
when it is rich and ripe –
let it be eaten with love
and the seeds planted
deep in the earth –
for another tree to grow –

I can't remember a time
when I didn't know you –
How many dreams ago
did I feel your warmth
in my first Teddy Bear
or hear your laughter
in the playground after school . . . . .
I have seen your eyes
in a magic cave
at Christmas
and remember you
in every holiday –
I think I must have known you
all my life –

THERE never was anyone like you –
You look at me
and I drown in your eyes –
You touch me
and my heart turns over –
You excite my mind
and fill my soul with peace –
Did I really exist before you
or was I just pretending
to be . . . . .

Dear chameleon,
you once told me
you changed
to the colour of me –
were you grey this morning
when you flew out of my life
into the sunrise?
the clouds were grey
and then the storm came –
I think the sky was angry
because you'd gone away –
dear chameleon,
what colour are you now?

ONCE I would have followed you,
begging you to let me in –
apologising for things
I'd never done,
gratefully accepting
your cold indifference
just to be near you –
I know better now –
but don't worry –
there will always be
another fool
to take my place –

You can have
money,
security
and love
taken from you –
but never
experience –

THE only measure
of my love
is your happiness –
even if
it is
with someone else.

It was a long time ago –
I was free
as usual –
so when you reached out
I was there –
available –
you – wearing your crumbling marriage
like an old soldier wears his medals,
me – with my need to be needed –
then I looked into your eyes,
beyond your own hurt,
I thought I saw the reflection
of a sad child –
so I crept away –
It was a long time ago . . . . .
why should you remember . . . . .

WHAT is to become of you
my friend?
Will you become a woman
or will you remain forever
a beautiful shell
that closes
at the first touch
of love . . . . .

Last seen
happily climbing
onto a golden horse
on the social merry-go-round –
I wonder if she'll get off
before it whirls her
into oblivion . . . . .

You fill your life
with empty conversation –
a self created vacuum –
a barrier of nothingness
built out of fear
that someone
might touch a scar
of yesterday –
Were you hurt too much
too young . . . . .
perhaps the wound
has never really healed . . . . .

THE glib, glossy people –
fabulous faces
and beautiful bodies –
who trade their souls
for the price
of a picture on a page,
a name on a silver screen
or the dull colour
of a dollar –
but where can a body go
without a soul?
perhaps hell is full
of fabulous faces
and beautiful bodies . . . . .

So what are you?
where have you been?
through a life
that never touched you –
a marriage
without love –
suffering loudly
but feeling no pain . . . . .
what do you want?
reward?
sympathy?
or an excuse
to make the next generation
feel guilty?

DIRTY politics,
dirty wars
and dirty money –
make the dirt
in my garden
seem so clean . . . . .

WHAT can I give
this beautiful new generation?
the unwanted gift
of my experience?
I don't think so –
perhaps only the right
to make the same mistakes
and afterward
not saying
"I told you so!"

Free, as the wind upon the ocean,
free, as a bird about to fly,
free, as a tiger in a jungle, –
freedom, that's the universal cry –
but do we cry
for freedom without thinking –
like a child wants everything he sees –
do we know that freedom can be lonely . . . . .
do we really have the courage
to be free?
Free, as a gypsy in the winter,
free, as a bird without a sky,
free, as a dolphin without water,
freedom –
that's the universal cry . . . . .

Pᴇᴏᴘʟᴇ of the theatre
disguise themselves
so cleverly,
so often –
no wonder
some of them forget
which one
they really are . . . . .

IT is a beautiful fact
that you and I together
can make one hour
into a holiday –

I knew her
when she was young,
beautiful
and full of dreams –
before he gave her children
without love –
before he broke her body,
her mind
and then at last her spirit –
they say she killed herself
last week –
I think she died
a long time ago . . . . .

In this world today –
so many people
searching for love
and truth
in the wrong places . . . . .

SOMETIMES, on a beautiful day
in early summer,
when the sun warms my body
and the rich, green grass
feels cool beneath my feet,
I watch the bees
go visiting the blossom
on a peach tree and wonder if,
like people,
busy gathering honey for the winter,
they often miss the spring . . . . .

I never could understand
what prompts people
to take a drug
to make the dawn
seem more enchanting –
or a sunset
outlive it's moment
of perfection –
I only know
the beauty God has created
is enough for me . . . . .

ALL those years –
looking for happiness
in someone else –
never quite daring
to search my own soul
in fear of what I might find –
then peace where I least expected –
the surprise of finding
I'm not as bad as I thought –

Fʀᴏᴍ the moment we find
pleasure in our own company,
we lose the fear
of growing old . . . . .

This Moment
is
Forever

In me,
there is an exquisite loneliness,
deep and personal
like unbearable pain –
I made friends with it
and found peace –

To share the night
and listen to the sound
of early morning traffic
in the street below –
to find the warmth
that lonely children dream –
and almost touch the sky –

SHE stood upon a rock
wondering if the waves
would take her
into the calm and shallow water
of some quiet lagoon –
or would they wash her off her feet
into a sea
where the ocean boils
with an excitement
so turbulent,
her body would surely drown
in the ecstasy –

Your warmth can melt
the brittle shell
around my heart –
then deep inside,
a tiny pulse becomes
the sound of drums –
I feel my soul reach out
to meet your own –
and you and I
become a symphony
of love –

I watched you sleeping –
How dare you be so beautiful?
your eyelashes brushing your cheek
with such easy familiarity
that I grow jealous of your face –
your lips half smiling
with the memory of the night –
It's time for you to wake,
but in all honesty,
I could no more disturb
the moonlit water on a summer night
or sunrise at the beginning
of a holiday . . . . .
How dare you be so beautiful?

I have loved you for so many years –
once in a while
the waves of my love
wash over the wall
of your self-protection
and almost reach your soul –
this is my reward.

So many times
I've glimpsed
another part of me
in strangers' eyes –
and so the game begins,
the touch –
the warmth –
the flame that burns too bright
and dies –
then comes the pain
that only friendship ends –

SOMETIMES,
through loneliness, pain
and too much responsibility
we come to know
the joy
of frivolity –

You think you love me –
so you shower me with gifts
and night and day,
extravagantly praise
the virtues
which I do not have –
but what is worse,
I accept your adulation
until our friendship
could dissolve
in utter self indulgence –

WHY is it so much harder
to accept the blame
for mistakes we **have** made,
than for those
we have not . . . . . ?

THERE are foolish people
who make work
into a terrible machine –
grinding away at life
until it disintegrates
in the dust
of duty . . . . .

SOMETIMES, I wonder
if the sick, commercial world
will eventually die of exhaustion –
before it destroys
humanity . . . . . ?

WHAT makes them
sit so close beside us
on the beach?
There is a whole great stretch of sand
for them to play upon –
Are they trying to be friendly –
or are they afraid
of each other's company?

Are the windows
of your mind so small,
you cannot see
what is going on
in the world outside?

Of all things
said or written,
perhaps one of the most beautiful is –
'the meek shall inherit the earth' –
but how long
can they remain meek
after they are given
the power and the glory?

THE only time
we have nothing at all
to fear –
is when we have nothing at all
to lose . . . . .

THEY enter my life
in one guise or another –
and I invite them in –
curiosity?
compassion?
sympathy? –
like guests
who stay too long,
they keep me
from loving . . . . .

HER soul watched
in helpless fascination
as the dark side
of her mind
led her body into hell –
and there together
in the evil glow,
her mind and body
watched her soul die –
in helpless fascination –

THERE is a breed
of nothing people
who live in a no – man's land,
somewhere between fear and truth –
their frustration makes them dangerous –
but only
to other nothing people –

PEOPLE seriously concerned
with saving other people's souls
often forget,
they too,
are only human beings . . . . .

WHEN the world crowds in
and makes my life seem small,
I break the barriers of reason
and fly to where you are –
so if I cannot find you,
please know I understand –
your world
is crowded too –

MAY the waters
where you live
be clear and calm
so you may see your way
up into the sunlight
of your mind –

She filled my house with flowers
and I helped her look for rainbows –
she understood so many things,
the importance of laughter
and that each moment is forever –
she dreamed impossible dreams,
smiled at strangers
because they might be lonely
and loved music, bells and butterflies
I'll think of her on sunlit days
and see her smile
in every flower . . . . .

To mourn too long
for those we love
is self indulgent –
but to honour their memory
with a promise
to live a little better
for having known them,
gives purpose to their life –
and some reason
for their death . . . . .

PLEASE give me time
to do the things
I have to do –
and a little more time
to do the things
I want to do –

Between Love
and
Loneliness

NANUSHKA
belongs to everyone
and yet to no – one –
perhaps that is why
this moment with you
is so very precious . . . . .

THERE was a time
when the world
was a great unopened thing, –
my eyes would feast
upon the gaudy paper,
my fingers trembled
on the coloured string –
so curious I was to find
those treasures
to satisfy my body,
those secrets
to excite my mind –
I opened it one summer
and wonder why, each Spring,
I never can replace,
exactly as it was,
the gaudy paper
and the coloured string . . . . .

I lost my way
in someone's eyes,
then reaching out
to touch a smile,
my heart became
a frightened butterfly –
we're lost together now,
my heart and I,
and only love
can find a way
from this sweet maze
of madness . . . . .

PLEASE do not take from me
this fragile cloak
of responsibility –
without it,
I am afraid
for both of us –

LAST winter
was walking in the rain –
lonely beaches,
the cry of a gull,
driftwood half buried
in the cold, wet sand
and the warmth
of you –
last winter
was rain on the roof,
firelight chasing shadows
on the ceiling
and loving –
last winter
was you . . . . .

In my mind
I love the taste
of life –
but in reality,
the sweetness
is often lost
in the confusion
of living . . . . .

. . . . . do you belong
somewhere at last –
are you happy –
do you hate me
for deserting you
or love me
for setting you free?
I only know
that strangers
wandering through my life
find unexpected love
because they remind me
of what we might have been . . . . .

BEAUTIFUL unlined faces,
like blank pages
waiting to be written upon –
eager young minds
thirsting for knowledge and truth –
healthy bodies
crying out for life and love –
they call it youth –
I remember it
as the confusion
of living somewhere
between heaven and hell . . . . .

W_{HY} fly so high
that dreams obscure the view
or run so fast
you miss the flowers
hidden in the early morning dew,
why take a crooked road,
forgetting which way's home,
or lose your zest for living
in a life that's not your own –
but come with me
and rest once in a while,
perhaps I recognise
the hurt and loneliness
that hides behind
your reckless smile . . . . .

You do not want
to face reality –
and every day
invent a little drama
of imaginary sorrow
or excitement
to pass the time away –
each has a happy ending
for your ego to enjoy,
sometimes you play the girl,
sometimes, the boy –
you are the martyr
and the hero
in your dreams,
and love is like a golden glow
to colour every theme –
I pray as time goes by
you'll see
the happiness and hurt and loving
life can **really** be –

SOMEWHERE in all of us
there is a someone
we mock, we fear
and do not want to know –
but once in a while,
if we are brave enough,
we must face
that frightening,
unknown clown
called 'self' –

You stood upon the brink of life
then stepped back
to join the empty, shallow people,
the vacuous faces
and venomous tongues,
the sad, confused sheep
they call society –
God help you from ever knowing
what you have missed
by not stepping forward –

We build
an image of ourselves
through sweat and tears –
but the idol falls
when it's feet of clay melt
in the sweat and tears
it was built upon –

In every crowded room
I search for you –
but when I see
your dear familiar eyes –
I turn away
for fear the world may see
the love
I never could
disguise . . . . .

WHEN loneliness
becomes a deafening bell,
so loud,
the world
will cover up it's ears –
when your heart cries out
for a friendly voice
and your mind could drown
in half forgotten tears –
you scream in silence
for an answer to your call
and in the empty echo
of your mind,
you know that you are human
after all
and that is consolation
of a kind . . . . .

ONE of the greatest crimes
one can commit
against society –
is to lose control
of one's self
in public.

LIVING so long
between a dream
and a nightmare –
it has taken
half a life time
to find
this precarious peace . . . . .

WHAT fools we are
to miss
the importance
of laughter –
the warmth
of understanding
and the gift
of friendship
that wait for us
between the extremes
of love and loneliness –

It is a sad fact
that people totally committed
to a political project
or a religious crusade,
are often such crashing bores,
they repel their converts
and can eventually destroy
the original seed
of their understanding –

WHEN we become good
at something –
there is no longer any reason
to tell people so –

It is so much better
to be a loser
and win –
than to be a winner
and lose –

PLEASE let me live
where honesty's a way of life
and people smile –
then offer you their friendship
without guile –
where strangers find a welcome
and no-one feels alone –
where I am loved
for being me
and not for what I own –

THANK God for Spring
when all the world is new again
and even gnarled old trees
wear coloured blossoms
on their scarred grey limbs
and reach the sky
to capture, once again,
a passing bird
or honey bee –

In time
we shall return
to purple hills
and yellow wildflower
in the valley –
to willows
rustling softly
in a summer breeze
and crystal waterfalls
that play their merry game
half hidden in a chuckling creek –
to scarlet breasted birds
chattering of their freedom
in the tops of cool, green trees
and all the sounds
that do not shatter silence
but are part of it . . . . .
in time
perhaps we'll learn
to live again . . . . .

Pocketful of Dreams

SOMEWHERE inside each of us
there are many different people –
perhaps Nanushka
is one of them . . . . .

I remember nights
when a lazy sea
lapped gently on silver sand –
I remember me,
brown and salty,
still warm from the morning sun,
drunk with living
and loving life
with a passionate innocence
which has never really left me . . . . .

Tumbling headlong
into life –
no regrets
from yesterday
or fears
for tomorrow –
saturating yourself
in today –
so why are you running
my young friend? –
this is where you live
now!

It is not your look
of knowing innocence
or the way you make me laugh –
it is not your gentle hands
or your warmth
that melts the winds of winter
in my heart –
it is so much more –
and yet perhaps I'll never know
what makes me love you . . . . .

O<small>NE</small> day,
it will be time
for you to leave –
I only hope
I love you enough
to let you go . . . . .

WE stole those precious hours
and spent them on each other,
like millionaires
with no tomorrow –
When you went away
you took a part of me –
please be gentle with it
and bring it with you
when you return –
I think it is my soul . . . . .

Too long
have I been the shore
and you, the sea –
bestowing gifts
of shells and driftwood
and gentle kisses
in the sun –
but when you roar
and beat me,
taking back your gifts
and leaving me exhausted,
I never know
if it is with love
or hate . . . . .

TAKE my body
if you must –
destroy my confidence
and deny me
my freedom –
but please,
leave me
my dreams –

I never did stop
loving **you** –
only what you have
become –

THERE comes a time
when all the troubles
of the world
seem unimportant
when pitted against the knowledge
that we, personally,
have only a limited time
to live . . . . .

We have the choice –
shall we allow
this life to become reality
without its two creators'
empty marriage vows?
Will this tiny human being
one day suffer for
the temerity of being born
or shall we destroy it before
it complicates some other life
already selfish to the core?
You were conceived in love
and not where duty lay –
you are your Mother's courage –
you are the seed of understanding –
let the world respect the child
who's born this way –

So little –
and the world's so big –

Have you ever wished to be
the very one you are –
have you ever tried to ski
a moonbeam to a star –
and have you dipped your fingers in
the rainbow's pot of gold
or watched the sky at daybreak
and seen a dream unfold?
for I have heard the raindrops laugh
and whisper 'How are you?'
and every day's like Christmas day
because of loving you –

SHE wrote
with simple innocence
about a world
that once she could not see –
she is a child
with beauty in her soul –
I offer her
my friendship –
and hope the cruel commercial world
will not destroy her spirit
or spoil the innocence
from which her great talent flows . . . . .

My God –
the confusion of youth –
the need for love
without the courage
to give entirely –
the dreams
without the will
to make them come true –
the pursuit of living
without understanding why –
the need for reassurance
and the constant search
for a purpose –
the people you miss
along the way –
until it is too late –
and youth is gone . . . . .

WHEN will society understand
that the most menial task
becomes an accomplishment
when it is done well –

JOHNNY's got a pocketful of dreams –
it's patched and there are cakecrumbs in the seams –
to you it may not be a lot
but all the treasure Johnny's got,
he carries in his pocketful of dreams –
a beetle in a match box, a tiny piece of string,
some sealing wax and carpet tacks,
a bell that doesn't ring –
When Johnny grows to be a man,
into a world that's tough,
he'll soon be told his pocketful of dreams
won't be enough –
but if he owns a great big car,
a swimming pool and yacht,
he'll never be as happy
as the time when all he's got
is a beetle in a match box, a tiny piece of string,
some sealing wax and carpet tacks,
a bell that doesn't ring . . . . .

If it became
the end of the world
and all the beautiful things
we have collected
in our life time
crumbled into dust –
and you and I survived,
what would we own?
only ourselves
and each other –
perhaps that is all we had
anyway . . . . .

It is a good idea
to learn to swim
before you try
to save a drowning friend . . . . .

I chose this way –
no-one beside me
to share the night
or find the day –
eating alone in restaurants,
reading books I've read before,
smilingly declining
to join dancers on the floor –
my eyes upon the pages,
my mind somewhere beyond,
you drink your coffee,
pay the bill –
in a moment you'll be gone –
I wonder if you feel the same –
did I really hope you'd stay?
and then I'm glad you didn't –
because like me,
you chose this way . . . . .

You wear your mask,
the friendly smile,
your warmth and welcome
bewitches for a while –
you make the old feel young,
the short feel tall –
I wonder if behind that bright facade
is there anyone at all? . . . . .

I stood between them,
felt their love flood over me,
melting the loneliness
that lives inside my soul –
their touch was warm
and welcome as winter sunshine –
for a moment they let me be
part of their loving –

Hollow eyed and deathly pale,
failing as only the desperate fail –
living in the mad extremes
of dull grey ache
and strange exotic dreams –
like a leaf in the Autumn wind,
sinning as only the pure can sin –
lost in a world of imperfection,
where is the life
and the resurrection?
Wanting to love, wanting to give,
living as only the lonely live . . . . .
A seed of love deep in your womb
grows in the dark
and dares to bloom . . . . .
and so in love and peace and warm
you're born again
as your child is born . . . . .

Every so often
I need you –
and somehow
you seem to know
that I do not need
your pity
but it seems to me
as though
you are waiting
for the funny,
complicated, loving me
to pour out
its wordless cries for help
that sometimes
only you
can see . . . . .

IF we do not
lose faith in ourselves –
there is a good chance
neither will anyone else . . . . .

OVER pale green velvet hills
into the dark rain forest –
dank leaves,
elusive waterfalls
and tangled creeper
blotting out the sky –
stumbling upward
to the patch of blue –
dappled sunlight
teasing butterflies –
then out into the clean sweet air
where birds,
with no regard for colour, kind or size,
fly free above the clouds
and you and I
can almost see forever –
we know we must return
the way we came . . . . . some time –
but knowing that it's there,
was worth the climb . . . . .

The Wonder
of
Tomorrow

SOMETIMES,
I wonder if love
is just a reflection
of ourselves
as we wish
we could be . . . . .

You are the music
for my words –
the other half of me –
perhaps one day,
together,
we'll become
a symphony –

I wonder
if I'll feel again
the ecstasy
that drowns out
common sense –
that takes away my conscience
and my strength –
shall I, just one more time,
forget that duty is enough –
throw caution to the winds
and give myself again
to love . . . . .

Last night
was warmth and laughter –
it was tenderness and tears
and eyes shining with love
like candles on a Christmas tree –
thank you –

You could explode with your loving –
or as easily,
melt into your own tears,
frustration welling up
like waves
from the turbulent ocean
of your soul –
perhaps you will drown
in your own passion
before it can be spent
on someone
unworthy of it . . . . .

A summer night
filled with peace –
you and I
wearing the warm
like a gossamer cloak
wrapped lovingly
in the wonderful sound
of silence . . . . .

I love you –
and yet
I do not presume
to know you –
your secret self
is a beautiful mystery
upon which
my heart
will not intrude –

How can we know
if this will last –
or shall I one day be
a misty memory
out of your past?
I only know
when I'm with you,
I feel that breathless hush
that comes before a storm is due –
and when you speak,
it seems to me,
I hear the strings
of some enchanted symphony
and so I'll stay,
this much I know –
to tell the truth,
my heart won't let me go . . . . .

It is easy
to be strong and brave
when I know
you are coming home –

LONELINESS
is being with you –
when you are thinking
of someone else –

I tried to remember the sea
when it was sparkling green
like an opal in the sun –
you lying on white sand
like a sleepy golden cat
with salt on your eyelashes –
but angry waves
crashed on to our beach
and the cold spray
filled my eyes and chilled my heart
until the memory disappeared
in a blur of salt and tears . . . . .

How can you
expect
anyone else
to love you
when you do not
even like
yourself?

It may be wise
to make our friends
before we make
our money –
or we may never recognise
our friends . . . . .

Why is it
the people
who claim to know us best –
are often those
who know us
least of all . . . . . ?

SURROUNDED
by moving mouths
and empty eyes –
listening to the senseless babble
of plastic people –
I wonder if their own noise
helps convince them
of their existence –

WHAT's to become of Mary Ann
twenty one today,
flying high but bound to fall,
not knowing why she's here at all –
and so afraid –
What's to become of Mary Ann
twenty two today,
eyes too bright or dull and glazed,
endless nights and longer days –
and so afraid –
What's to become of Mary Ann
twenty three today,
buying minutes free from pain,
raddled face and addled brain –
and so afraid –
What's to become of Mary Ann
nearly twenty four,
existing in her twilight gloom,
dying in some dirty room –
and so afraid –

DEMOCRACY
would work,
if only
people
liked each other
a little more –

You – with your intuition –
your dream of glory without power –
will the people stand beside you –
shall we share your finest hour?
Are you too close to us to help us
because you feel the way we feel –
are you too much human being,
is this your Achilles heel?
You have the courage and integrity
and perhaps you'll prove it true –
you can be a politician
and a human being too –

WHAT a pity
so many people
confuse peace
with boredom . . . . .

It is sad to watch.
those busy, commercial bees –
do they think
they can sting humanity
into an awareness
of their own importance?

You were the seed
flung in anger by a storm –
you sheltered by the gnarled old tree
to find the warm –
and there you grew
beside your newfound friend,
perhaps a little wild,
not knowing why or to what end –
but as the old tree bowed
to sun and wind and time,
you lovingly adorned your dying friend
with fresh green leaves and flowers
to make a youth and wisdom shrine –
and when the Autumn winds grow cold,
the countryside is bleak and bare,
you will be shelter for another seed,
flung by the storm
into your care –

HE came from the people
who worship the earth –
you were his world
and his dreamtime –
now his spirit has returned
to some distant place
to live forever
in peace and friendship
with his own people –
and you have inherited
the beautiful memory
of his loyalty and loving –

I looked
at old photographs today
and saw myself
young and beautiful,
vain, self-centred
and confused –
I wondered why anyone
should mind
growing older
and wiser . . . . .

It does not matter
if we look old –
as long as
we think young –

WE painted the sunrise
and made us a day –
we sang us a summer
from June until May –
we coloured each moment
with laughter and warm
and wrote us a sunset
that lasted till dawn –
but dreams and schemes and holidays
must always have an end,
so thanks for the ride on the rainbow
my friend –

My greatest wish
is for those
I have loved
to find someone
worthy of them –

With grateful thanks to Bruce Swann
for his sketches and his understanding
of Nanushka's thoughts.